LAMBENT LIGHT

Who Will Know Their Name?

ASH ADAMS

WESTBOW
PRESS®
A DIVISION OF THOMAS NELSON
& ZONDERVAN

WestBow Press books may be ordered through booksellers or by contacting:

WestBow Press
A Division of Thomas Nelson & Zondervan
1663 Liberty Drive
Bloomington, IN 47403
www.westbowpress.com
844-714-3454

Scripture quotations are from the ESV® Bible (The Holy Bible, English Standard Version®), Copyright © 2001 by Crossway, a publishing ministry of Good News Publishers. Used by permission. All rights reserved.

ISBN: 978-1-6642-6114-3 (sc)
ISBN: 978-1-6642-6115-0 (hc)
ISBN: 978-1-6642-6113-6 (e)

Library of Congress Control Number: 2022905114

Print information available on the last page.

WestBow Press rev. date: 04/19/2022

CONTENTS

PART 4

ACKNOWLEDGMENTS

Let me first remember that this was produced in God's strength, and for that I give Him my praise and thanks. I extend a huge thank you to Stephanie Erickson, author of over twenty books, who encouraged me so much with my initial pamphlet draft. Because of her, this book has grown. Further cause for thanks is Ruth Buchanan, author and teacher now teaching others to write through Buildabetterus.com.

I am thankful for all the helpful comments from all my Beta readers.

INTRODUCTION

Dear Reader,

You are holding a book that is precious because it has a purpose. If this was a biography, it would be much longer; nevertheless, I have included much of my background to tell the story, so that you may get to know me and understand me better.

This book shows how God was always in my life—I was just too blind to see. I want most of all to encourage every reader to stop and look for that same lambent light that is always around me and you. It took me a long time to see that light, and maybe I can help you to be more observant than I was.

The book tells of how I lived as a child and kept secrets, how I lived and worked as an adult and kept secrets, and how God held me through it all. It is not easy to expose things that I chose to keep private, even though I now have an explanation for many of the events that happened and that seemed weird to me at the time. Some were not good, but just because I am writing about them makes them no worse. We all know we cannot undo the past, but we can stop bad memories from taking up residence in our minds, and adversely affecting our present and our future. We can choose. We sometimes give too little credit to the power of our minds. We can dwell on the past or choose to see the joys of life. Our thoughts make all the difference, but those of us who are Christ-followers also have the help of the Holy Spirit and the strength of God. Our real power comes from God.

Thank you for choosing this book. My prayer is that God's hand guided you to it because He wants you to see the lambent light.

PART 1

CHAPTER 1

As you enter these memories

There was a time when I did not know God. It was a long time. It was a very long time—more than half my life. There was also a time when I had never heard the word *lambent*. This adjective describes a light or fire that is glowing or flickering with a soft radiance. As soon as I heard it, the word grabbed my attention. The more I thought about it, the more I saw that God is our lambent light: glowing, gleaming, or flickering, with that soft radiance.

Bathed in this light, I feel warm and safe.

"Again Jesus spoke to them, saying, 'I am the light of the world. Whoever follows me will not walk in darkness, but will have the light of life'" (John 8:12). This scripture is very familiar, and I now read it with the awareness that God is my lambent light. I especially note the words "will not walk in darkness." Because this lambent light is always there, we can have the opportunity to never walk in darkness if only we would accept God's gift.

However, I can see that God used stronger beams of light to try to make me notice Him. It was as if He was sending rays of light from a lighthouse to direct my path. I didn't even notice. As I said, it took a while. True to His word in Jeremiah, God had plans for me, "plans for welfare and not for evil, to give you a future and a hope" (Jeremiah 29:11). These words are often quoted, and they speak of God's wisdom and encouragement to us.Through Jeremiah, God was talking to the

Israelites and teaching them of His plans for their nation. He was repeating His promise to them. They were descendants of Abraham, with whom God had made a covenant, and God was not going to break His side of this bargain. Of course, the covenant foretells of the coming of Jesus. When scriptures become as familiar as this one, we can deduce their full meaning. God has indeed made plans for each of us.

In this book, you will find a collection of God stories. These stories are experiences in which God was clearly in control, and sometimes the only explanation for why things happened the way that they did.

As I have said, there was no visible bright, flashing light accompanying each event. In retrospect, I now see that these experiences acted as guiding lights as if from a lighthouse, leading me away from the rocks and toward a safe harbor. That was then. Now I have God as a permanent lambent light around me, and I sense that is exactly how He asks us to be around each other.

As you enter these memories, you will perhaps notice and develop a sense of that lambent light. That is my hope.

If we were sitting across from one another having a coffee instead of meeting through pages like this, you would no doubt have noticed my accent by now. Though I am currently a permanent resident of the United States, I am from England. It amuses me that some official references call me an alien. As I write this, I have been in the States for over seven years and have enjoyed the benefits of life in Florida. I enjoy the sun. I love the fact that we all think we speak the same language, and yet I have made many errors by using words differently from the Americans. Sometimes that has been funny and sometimes embarrassing.

God has had plans for me for sure—plans I could never have imagined. Without my awareness, or approval, God has decided my path. And now that I know more of God and His nature, I can rest in full assurance that He is always at work. What comfort! I hope as you read on, you will see that these events that I want to share can only be explained as interventions from God. But first let me tell you of my beginnings. Let me tell you what I was like and maybe you can see why I was so self-governing, so blind to God.

CHAPTER 2

As if we were dead to each other

I start with the premise that my family was odd. I needed to understand that, since I found it hard to believe the degree of oddness. I can look back now with the eyes of an adult, and see that I had no sense of family. The sad thing is that maybe I omitted to instill this in my own children, even though I loved both my sons so much.

I know we are supposed to learn from our trials, but I prefer this verse from Rebecca McCann.

They say our hardships help us grow

And make us strong and wise

But if there's one thing I dislike

It's blessings in disguise. (McCann, 1960, page50)

The number of the house where I lived from the age of two until I was sixteen was 192. It was a three-bedroom terraced house in the county of Kent in the south of England. My mother was one of nine children and her mother had died in childbirth. She married my father and they had five children.

I was born in the northeast of England but when I was about two, we moved to the county of Kent. This was a move from one end of England to another. We moved from one culture to a very different culture. In the northern mining village where we had lived, people did not lock their front doors and neighbors would just walk into your house. This was not the case in the south; the doors were always locked and one would ring a doorbell if one visited. My mother was born in that northern village but my father was born in Yorkshire—still in the north but farther south.

People born in the northeast are called Geordies, and they have a unique accent. We must have been too young to have picked up the dialect. The way of life in the northeast is very different too. At the time of our move, the main industry was coal mining. My uncle worked in the mines, much to the detriment to his health. Up north, people are more outspoken and speak their minds very freely. Down south, people are less open. Often, as an adult, I would wake in the early hours of the morning with a sudden understanding of what someone who had spoken to me previously had meant for me to hear. People in the south go all around the houses to say things instead of just speaking plainly.

I had no idea why we moved to this house, number 192. I can only assume it was related to my father's employment opportunities. At that time, I had two older brothers, Tony and John; later, my younger brother Philip and sister Carol were born. My mother always referred to us as "the three big ones" and the "two little ones."

There was nothing good about 192, and as a result I have always used the word "one-nine-two" as an adjective to describe anything that reminded me of the place. I have a mental list of things that I no longer give any place in my life. I will group the list, which is by no means conclusive, but each set gives an idea of how I viewed things.

- Plum jam
- Only having one choice of jam
- Margarine
- Watery custard
- Boiled fish

Certain food items are listed. We always had only one of everything. We were fed bread and jam many times, and for some reason it was always plum jam. There was never a choice. There was never a change of flavor. We (the children) always had margarine, but I noticed my mother would serve herself butter. I decided that if my entire family could not have butter, then we would all have margarine. Thoughts like this were never uttered, of course. Our custard was always so watery that it just was not custard; it was tasteless and diluted. It was like the pastry on the weekly apple pie: never golden brown and appetizing, just pale and half-baked. Then there was the boiled fish. We had a pet cat who was fed boiled fish, as were we. The smell permeated the house for a start, but the pale, sad fish for us or the cat offended me, even at such a young age.

- Salmon pink (the color)
- Eiderdowns
- Floral furnishings
- Bathroom doors with no locks
- Stairs that creak
- Ticking clocks

This bunch connects me to my bedroom, and sex abuse. I had salmon pink furnishings; the eiderdown quilt on the bed and the curtains were both floral. I could hear a ticking clock in my parent's bedroom as I waited to see if my father would make that dreadful creak on the stairs, coming to me. I hated, too, that I could not lock the bathroom door because as I grew older my father could, and would, walk in on me at any time.

I was very critical about how the house looked.

- Curtains that did not meet in the middle
- Unused front rooms
- Allocated seating
- Light bulbs that were dim
- Linoleum floor covering
- Magnolia-colored paint

Every room was painted the same color, and every room had curtains that did not fit the windows. They never met when pulled together and were faded and thin. Our lights were almost a misnomer since they gave little illumination. Maybe because of my vision loss it bothered me, but I do not know. We had a front room that was only used on Christmas Day. There were seven of us in a three bedroom terrace house, and yet one room could not be used. It baffled me. Of course, nobody questioned this out loud. We also had limited carpeting, so our feet would get cold on the old, cracked linoleum flooring. In a way, the next group continues the theme of how things were in the house.

- Being cold
- Rough towels
- Dirty ornaments
- Stained cups

I am describing a place devoid of comfort. I was always cold. If it was time to light the fire, it was a meagre defense against the permanent chill. Too many people were trying to reach some warmth. Getting washed was awful because we had limited hot water. Any wash was as quick as one could make it, and finished off with rough towels. I noticed the dirt on ornaments (household decorations) and the tea stains in the cups, and I hated them. All these things itemized give only a glimpse of the things I call one-nine-two.

- Hands round my neck
- Being called by my full name
- Pinnies (aprons)
- My hair parted in the center
- Hair ribbons

My parents each had an armchair beside the fireplace. We children would sit on the rug on the floor or at the dining table.

My mother was always in a pinny, as we called aprons. She was the only person who always called me by my full name. Hearing my full name always now fills me with a sense of foreboding. For some reason, my mother wanted my hair parted in the middle and a ribbon tied around it. I have no idea why I seem to overreact to anyone putting their hands around my neck. I have no memories of any event that may have instilled this fear, and yet it exists in a very strong way.

My family was dysfunctional. I use the words *home, family, parent, mother,* and *father,* but none of them describe the place I lived in or the people I lived with. I have very few memories of my brothers and sisters when we were young; however, I do remember that we were all treated differently. My mother had an overdeveloped idea that my eldest brother, as her first born, was particularly special and therefore favored by her. He would be fed a cooked meal every evening while the rest of us had bread and jam. This changed when my second brother passed the exam for the grammar school. Life then revolved around his homework. My eldest brother became increasingly identified as the troublemaker. I always felt safe when he was around, but everyone else seemed frightened of him. I have scant memories of my younger brother and sister. Philip was skinny and seemed scrawny, and he did not do well at school. My sister Carol, when she was a baby, cried and cried. Often, I had to take her out for walks in her pram (baby carriage).

These are the sorts of things that did make an impression. I saw that they were wrong. My father scared me, and with good reason. He sexually abused me until I left home, and he physically beat my eldest brother.

I said earlier that I can now see how ungrateful and critical I seem to have been. In my defense, I can see that I never saw or felt any love. A child who was loved may have learned a sense of forgiveness and sympathy. Even before I saw that things for other people were different, I seemed to know that my situation could be better.

Seven of us lived in this small house, apparently unaware of what was going on around us, or of what was happening to any of the others. I suppose I was just locked into my own world. I was very, very young when I learned that I had no one to communicate with—no one, that is, who shared my level of awareness, no one who wanted to talk. A knowledge of the meaning of aloneness came upon me at this time.

I had a friend, Julie, who was an only child, and she used to envy me because I had brothers and a sister. I could never understand this because, whenever I was in her house, I seemed to be surrounded by noise and chatter in which I was both included and involved—and there were only three people in her family. This household was a very different place compared to the activities of 192, where I wasn't convinced that anyone knew I existed most of the time.

Many people look back fondly on their childhood years as a time of warmth and safety, but I do not. I used to think that maybe I was adopted. If I am honest, I sometimes wished I would be swooped up by some caring person who would tell me she was my real mother but had lost me, and who had suddenly found me again.

In my house, there was no communication, no chat, and no banter. By the time I was seven years-old, I knew I had to leave the house. I could go on, but as I write, I get a visual memory of all these things and how I used to think. I look at seven-year-olds today and cannot quite believe that they are capable of thinking the way I did at that age.

I had no feeling of love toward my parents; it was as if we were dead to each other. In fact, I did not feel parented in any way. Instead, I felt tended. I was fed and watered and allowed to keep growing. My life was about being out of the house as much as possible. I learned to just block off what was happening. I compartmentalized my life: I was inside or outside, it was daytime or it was nighttime. If I was inside, I was either doing chores or reading. If I was outside during the day, then I was either running to the local shops for my mother, or I was free to play with my friends. I felt like I was invisible. No one ever asked if I was okay, and I discovered very early on that it was pointless to ask for anything. If I was outside playing, only when the other mothers called their children would I know it was time to go home. If I was inside and it was nighttime, I would be dreading the sound of my father's footsteps on the stairs—and rightly so because he sexually abused me until I was sixteen. This abuse I knew was not right. I knew it was wrong and by no means normal. How did I know that? At such a young age? I just did. I have no memory of being told not to tell anyone, yet I told no one. I suppose I knew I would not be heard.

The effect of the abuse on both my brother and myself has been lifelong. As a child, I was trapped and scared and longed to be removed from that house. I used to daydream in class about how I would be amazingly rescued. Bit of a drama queen, do you think? As I grew, I feared becoming pregnant. What on earth would happen if I did? I had no clue. After I left home, I expected to get over it all, but instead I found that I had flashbacks. The timing of these was random. I could be walking along the street and suddenly find myself reliving the experiences, even to the point of a physical sensation of my father on top of me. I would have to stop walking and gather myself, and then carry on with whatever I was doing. These stopped in my mid-forties as a result of my telling a friend all about it. Fortunately for me, she had counselling experience and helped me to divulge all the sordid details—not once, but many times, and as a result the effect of the abuse became minimized. It was not unimportant, but smaller in impact, if that makes sense.

Years later, after my divorce, I visited my elder brother and he told me about his abuse. I knew he was often beaten but I did not know what he did to cope. He told me he would sneak out of the house, before our father came home, and go into the garage of a good friend. One night his friend's father discovered my brother trying to sleep on the floor. What happened next made me cry. Without asking any questions, he gave my brother a key to the house and told him to sleep on the sofa any time he wanted to. Isn't that wonderful?

Yet it shows that no adult would take any action with any of the authorities at that time. Next it was my turn to cry, as I told my brother what happened to me. I did not cry until my brother cried for me. It was the only time anyone had cared so much.

My brother spent so much time trying to get his father to show love to him, but it never happened. He even housed my father, and the man just wrecked the house. As for me, I may now see that my mother had a hard life, but I cannot believe she did not know what was happening to me or explain why she offered me no protection at all. I say that as a mother, who heard her sons every time they turned over in bed, just about.

The effect on me hits in other ways too. Sometimes, it would surprise me. As a nurse, I came to realize that when I was dealing with a case of child abuse from a mother, I would be seeking help and support for her. However, if the child was harmed by the father, I would want to see him punished. At least I came to recognize the prejudice that I had. I can remember a few years after I had become a Christian noticing how a man was reacting to his child. I was astonished to see that he clearly loved that child very much. I had assumed men could not love children as mothers can. As a result, I know sex abuse is a particular crime. I believe only those who have suffered from it understand this. It is not child rape. It is not sexual. It is perversion. Here is the awful confession: as a Christian, I believe that God can do the impossible, *but* sadly I feel that sex abusers of children do not get God's attention.

CHAPTER 3

I was playing the wrong game

My earliest memory is of my first day at school—and that I cried. The class was told to draw a picture of their favorite nursery rhyme, but I didn't know what a nursery rhyme was. I knew the rhyme but not that it was called a nursery rhyme. This particular event had such an effect on me that I resolved to try to never assume that my own children would know what things were called. As a result, when they were tiny I used to say, "this is a cup," "this is a fairy story," "this is a game," to the point of absolute craziness.

I went to hospital twice when I was young. The first visit was for a tonsillectomy, but the second was a slow realization that things were bad. I had broken my leg in an accident in the local park. A new piece of equipment had been installed called a rocking horse. It had a head and tail separated by a bench of seats. All the children lined up to take a turn. There were pushers at the front and pushers at the back. After every turn, we all would move up a position. It became my turn to lead the back pushers. Suddenly, I slipped and my legs shot under the horse, and it came down onto one of my legs bearing the weight of about four children. I probably screamed because I remember being taken to hospital in the back of a neighbor's van and my leg hurting. The next thing I remember was travelling home in an ambulance with my whole leg in plaster. From then on, a sort of war started between my father and me as he persisted in carrying me everywhere when I wanted to walk. As he carried me, he was touching me where I did not want to be touched. It took me about four more years to wake up to what was happening to me.

When I was seven years old, I learned I would have to stay in school until I was sixteen. This meant that I could not leave home until then, but I decided I would leave on my sixteenth birthday. I look at seven-year-old children now and see how small they are and how childlike, and I wonder that I could make such a firm resolution at such an innocent age. I wonder what today's seven-year-olds are really thinking. It never dawned on me to reevaluate my decision; it never dawned on me to tell anyone, and it never occurred to me to run away. I must have assumed I would somehow survive until this magic day when I would be free to go. Life went on, but the only good times were now had out of the house, either at school or, increasingly, as I grew older, playing with my friends outside.

My mother had a set day for every job and a set meal to go with it. I could tell what day of the week it was by either the meal at lunchtime or the housework my mother was doing. Monday was always cold roast lamb and mashed potatoes. If it was not raining then the wash could hang outside to dry, and then the afternoon would be spent starting the ironing. This was done by my mother, who had to heat, and constantly reheat, a small, solid iron on the gas cooker (stove). By the time I was considered old enough to help, we had an electric iron. I always found our ironing board too thin for the task and we never had a proper cover for it. Old sheets were used to pad the surface instead, but since these dangled down they inevitably got in the way and so impeded progress. On Tuesdays, my mother would clean downstairs with an old cylinder vacuum cleaner. However, this seemed to make the job harder rather than easier, so she ended up using the broom most of the time.

On Wednesdays, there was more ironing; Mother would also get a small amount of shopping at the nearest parade, or row, of shops to us called The Oval. By the time I was ten years old, I was expected to do errands as well. My mother always referred to my shopping jobs as either errands or running messages—I noticed that my friends' mothers would just call it going to the shops. Thursday was the big shopping trip, which was always done in the afternoon.

Sundays were spent cooking the roast lamb, roast potatoes, and cabbage. The cabbage was watery and soggy, yet I liked it. Years later, I found out just how delicious it could be if cooked less and served with butter and black pepper. To accompany the apple pie, always referred to as afters (dessert) in our house, was thin, watery custard. At least it helped the pastry go down, and for us it was the norm. As my world expanded and I was invited out to friends' houses, I began to see that things could be better and brighter, and I increasingly compared 192 to others unfavorably.

This was my life situation. I went into the junior school, where I was so often called by my brothers' names in place of my own, especially by the headmaster. I cannot remember that children were naughty at school—except for the day I misbehaved. We were all being taken outside to sit on the grass to watch some event which I cannot recall now. All I know is that we were all excited about it, including me. There we were, a line of ten-year-olds sitting cross-legged expectantly, as others joined us. Idly I picked a piece of grass and began to chew it. The teacher told me to take it out of my mouth, which I did. However, I put a fresh piece in again and she asked me to stop, only this time adding that if she caught me again I would be sent inside. Despite the fact that that was the last thing I wanted, and despite the fact that I knew she would carry out her threat, I chewed again. As predicted, I was caught and sent back to the classroom. I can remember watching from the window, which was no fun at all, and asking myself why I had disobeyed. I still have not a clue.

The headmaster was called Mr. Warren, and he used to take us once a week for a very different sort of lesson. We never knew what the subject would be, and there was always the chance to earn commendations which, up until then, had only been given for written work. I always got commendations for my work. I always sat at the front of the second row in the class. We had not been able to choose where we sat but had found our names on our desks on the first day. One day, we had been learning lots of long words, which Mr. Warren wrote on the blackboard until it was completely covered with column after column of them. He asked us to stand along the back wall of the classroom, and when he pointed to a word, we had to pronounce it, explain what it meant, and then close our eyes and spell it. I used to love things like this and was usually quite good at it; however, little did I know that I was playing the wrong game. When it was my turn, he had got to the top of the third column and suddenly I realized I could not remember which word was there. I went through the list again, but it was no use; I just could not recall the word. Mr. Warren then realized I was trying to do it all from memory and said I was just to read the word.

"But I can't see the word from here," I said. I could not believe that any of us could actually see those words well enough to read them. I had always thought the test was about memory, when in fact it was just easy-peasy reading. How thick can one get? I was prescribed glasses shortly afterwards.

It was in Mrs. Bud's class that I started to have frequent gumboils, which I presume was caused by a poor diet and lack of dental hygiene. While these gumboils did not embarrass me, I did notice that nobody else seemed to have them, and you could not help but notice as my mouth and face swelled. One of these gumboils once covered my two front teeth, which gave the teacher the impression that I was eating a sweet. She ordered me to take the sweet out of my mouth and would not accept my explanation until she actually looked inside my mouth. The next thing I knew, I had to attend the school dental service, and at that tender age I lost many of my lower molars through dental extraction. It is little wonder that in later years, my own children were made to clean their teeth. I followed through and did not just assume they were doing it. I also restricted their sugar intake and ensured they had fluoride toothpaste. How proud I was when, in their teens, they announced that they were the only ones in their respective classes who had no fillings. They even asked, "What are fillings, Mum?"

Julie, my friend who wished she had brothers and sisters, and I became inseparable friends. We spent most of our time at the golf links. It was dissected by a rambling stream, and our best fun was had jumping the river. There were set places to jump because the stream had tiny beach-like patches to jump onto. Some of the jumps were much harder than others, and I was less able and less confident than Julie. If anyone got her feet wet, it would be me and there were many a day that I squelched home. Wouldn't you have thought that my mother would have noticed and made a comment? But I was never in trouble for it. Odd. If I squelched to Julie's house, I would get a hot drink and a biscuit or something, while my socks dried. My sandals would then be stuffed with paper and put outside to dry before I went home.

It is no wonder that I began to notice that other families lived differently to us. All the time I was making decisions about how I would do things when I grew up: we would not have the same meals every week on the same day; all of my family would eat the same food at each meal time; I would like my children and talk to them and play with them. I would always want to know where my children were, and if they were in trouble I would stick up for them. No wonder I felt invisible. Nobody ever asked what I was doing or where I was going when I went out. Nobody ever called me in for bedtime either, but once our friends had been called there was nothing left to do but go home and go to bed to read. I read and reread every book I owned. I would read anything I could get my hands on.

I remember the coronation of the present Queen for two reasons. The first is that it coincided with the arrival of an invitation for me to be a bridesmaid at the wedding of Auntie Eva's only son, my cousin Richard. The second memory is that we did not have a television, so I was invited to spend the whole day watching Julie's television. I knew this was going to be as good as a two-week holiday: to have a whole day being a part of things *and* watching television *and* seeing the coronation. I have no idea what the rest of my family did.

CHAPTER 4

I was not prepared in any way for this

Before the wedding, I was to sit the eleven-plus exam. Every child took this exam when he or she was around eleven years-old. I was to be eleven at the end of the school year. The exam decided if one went to a grammar school or the local secondary modern, as it was called. If you went to the grammar school, you were considered capable of doing harder academic work. As far as I am aware, I was not prepared in any way for this. I was not even aware that I was sitting it. I went to school as usual and just accepted the different instructions, doing each test as it was presented to me. I did recognize that the spelling test was different; for a start, it did not center on that week's word list, which was always written on the blackboard under the category "Extra Work," to be done in class whenever you found yourself with time to spare. Doing extra work earned commendations, so I paid attention to it. However, this particular spelling test was much longer and there were adults, strangers I think, walking around the classroom looking at what we had written. Gradually, children's papers were removed and I was aware that there were only a few of us left. My paper was taken away after I had tried to spell the word *eggsagerate*. I wonder how many others had got it wrong.

Only afterwards did I find out what was happening when all of us were talking and I realized it was being called the eleven-plus. I thought no more about this until the results came. If I am right, I think we were given letters to take home at dinnertime. I don't think the school told us the content of the letters. Anyway, I dutifully took mine home and was told I had passed the eleven-plus. There was no celebration or anything. I might just as easily have been told it was raining. Tony and John were out at their respective schools, and I had never even asked why they went to different places. I was so thick (so slow to notice).

It was not until I got back to school that I realized that passing the eleven-plus had been some sort of achievement which ought to especially please me. Two children were missing from school, and others had been obviously crying. I can remember wondering what could have happened that I did not know about, and having a feeling of uneasiness. Julie told me she had passed and asked if I had. She was thrilled to bits when I told her I had because it meant we could go on being friends. I could not see why, if I failed, we would stop being friends, but then Julie was always ahead of me when it came to understanding the consequences of things.

Some time after this, we had to select our options for which grammar school we wanted to attend. Before that term ended, all the parents were invited to the new school to learn all about it. The following day, my mother sat me down, thrust a piece of paper in my hands, and said, "Read that, and don't ever let a boy touch you there." This was my introduction to menstruation and the only sex lesson I ever had. It was Julie who told me how babies were born. I can see myself now so full of awe at this revelation. I asked Julie in a hushed voice, "Does the Queen do it?"

By the time I left junior school, I was a confusion of personalities. There was the happy me at school, finding it easy to be successful and have friends. There was the *outside me* who could play outside with friends knowing I had so much to learn from them, knowing they did things differently in their houses. If I silently watched, I could absorb all those differences and store them away until I needed to know about them. Their tables were set differently and were always more full of food than ours. Their curtains seemed to fulfil a purpose; their houses seemed less dark. There was a sense of home, whereas I felt I lived in a house. The *inside me* was very critical of 192, and intensely watchful of everywhere else. I knew I would be leaving, but I still had a few years to go.

For most of my life, I did not know God. I knew *of* God because at school we were told stories from the Bible. This knowledge did not apparently have an impact on me at all. However, God was even there, ensuring I received a foundation of knowledge, and ensuring I heard the name Jesus. This too was part of that lambent light, and the Holy Spirit would later teach me more.

By the time I grew up, I decided that people who went to church were just different. When you are a child, of course, whatever your family does, most of the time but not always, feels like the norm. It seemed strange to me that people would go to church. Our family did not do so, and for that reason, I had no clue why people went there. In my world, God had nothing to do with our lives at all. I did not understand that going to church had any purpose. I had also decided that the Pope was pompous and the Roman Catholic church was my idea of exactly why I could never enter churches with statues of Mary, Jesus on the Cross, and angels. That was religion with a capital R.

Of course, God had His hand on my life.

"As your days, so shall your strength be" (Deuteronomy 33:25). As you read, you will discover why this scripture has become my go-to verse. God carries us through. In my view, sex abuse is a particular crime. No one can understand how it feels. They think they can, but they cannot. I say this because of the way society reacts. I believe things have improved, but a judge in England once announced that a nine-year-old little girl "asked for it," after she was raped. I believe pedophiles exist in all areas, and in all professions; as a result, those who are supposed to protect us actually perpetuate the crime. Society recognizes this, yet there are no effective or efficient checks and balances in place. I can now see that God gave me coping mechanisms. For example, during the abuse, I would concentrate on my homework timetable and mentally check off all the assignments we had been given—just blocking off events again. I did not have the language to give this abuse a name, and yet I instinctively knew it to be wrong.

This is a powerful witness to the character of our God. God always gives us strength to get through each day, no matter what happens. I hope as you read on, you will see that through all of my life, God has been a flickering light, carefully keeping me at His side. I, of course, had no idea or sense of His presence. Is this the same for you?

It was during the summer holidays, when I was ten, that I was invited back up north to be a bridesmaid for a cousin I did not know at all. I was put on a train, all alone, for the six-hour ride. I was to stay for the whole six-week summer holiday, until term restarted at my new school. This visit was an eye-opener. For the first time in my experience, I was living in a family and being treated as if I were loved. I met my aunt and uncle, my cousin, and his fiancée.

CHAPTER 5

I did not know they were mine

My aunt, who I came to adore, told me one day, about a week after I had arrived, that I was an odd child. When I asked her why, she said that there were sweets in the drawer, and I had never taken one. She did not know a child who did not like sweets. My reply was, "I did not know they were mine!" I was then informed that they were not mine; they were for anybody and everybody. I was told, in fact, I could have anything in the house—without asking! It seemed odd to me. I tested this. My aunt made delicious bilberry pies, and I helped myself to the biggest slice. My aunt saw this and yet she said nothing. I helped myself again. Oh, she really *meant* it. I could have anything.

The wedding happened and my bridesmaid dress was made by my aunt, who was a tailor. There was one hitch: she decided to get my hair permed, and it became a frizzy mess—and I had to wear a ribbon. This horrified me, but I did not mind because I was so loved. The newlyweds really almost adopted me, and every time I could, I would return to holiday with them, taking some of my friends too.

This first visit was the most enjoyable time of my childhood. I made friends. I had new experiences and new freedoms—and no abuse. I was sad to leave and return home, but somewhat overawed at the prospect of a new school and the bus ride to reach it. I, in fact, took two different bus rides. I travelled with my friend Julie, the one who envied me. We lived on the same road and used the same bus-stop, but she had a free-fare-pass from the council because she lived the required distance from the school; apparently, I did not. I can understand now why this rankled my mother, but at the time I just wondered why she could not just put up with it. I seemed to go through life just getting on with whatever was in front of me, as if all feelings were numbed.

In grammar school, we were taught to discuss and understand, not necessarily to agree. I always feel I had an education rather than a schooling. By that I mean that we were exposed to a wide variety of topics, whereas today it seems that children are schooled to pass tests. Schools are judged by their test results, rather than on the progress of the children. The two are not the same. I was introduced to a broad range of the sciences and arts, whether I appreciated them or not at the time. Fortunately, I found school fairly easy and enjoyed it because it gave me a reason to be out of the house. That is also why I joined every school society that I could. They often met after school and I could stay behind and delay returning home. My short visit to my aunt and uncle had confirmed in me that there was another way to live. My life was not normal after all, and I learned that I, in fact, had no family. I lived in a house full of people of a variety of ages who were totally unconnected except biologically. I seem to have just accepted the situation I was in and, although I knew I would leave 192 as soon as I could, I also was aware that I was legally expected to attend school. It never occurred to me that I could run away. I think I have told you how slow I can be to work things out sometimes.

By the time I left school, I needed work that would give me a roof over my head. This led me to consider nursing, since back then nurses were required to be in residence for their entire training, with their board and lodging deducted from their pay. To bridge the gap until I was old enough to start my training, I worked as a care assistant at a Church of England residential school for handicapped children. This large house was where the children and staff lived. The school was a separate building on the grounds. The children were periodically reviewed by a visiting orthopedic surgeon from a London hospital. This is where I decided to train.

PART 2

CHAPTER 6

Life could be different

Before I knew God, I would have told you I simply had no interest in Him. I was indifferent. It was as if God had passed me by. I had the same view about other things, such as horse riding or cooking—they just had not figured in my life. They did not matter to me. Much later, I would read in the Bible that this indicated that I had a hard heart and thus hated God. Since I did not feel hate, I found that scripture difficult. But as I think more logically, I can see why this is true.

Most people, possibly, think that the opposite of love is hate. In fact, the opposite of love looks like indifference. You know, dog owners know their pets love them, whereas cats sometimes act as if their owners are on the staff. If we are loved, we feel it; if we are hated, we feel it; if anyone is indifferent to us, we feel that absence. If someone loves us and we show indifference, it is worse than showing hate. Indifference is not a position of neutrality.

I have come to realize the full weightiness of God's command to love one another as He loves us. Thus indifference, to Him, is a sin. To be indifferent is to care less. When I was young, I couldn't have cared less about God, yet He could not have cared more about me.

As I think back, I can see so clearly now that God did indeed have plans for me, and that His plans have brought me nothing but blessings. How He must have despaired at some of the things I thought and said. Nevertheless, He gave me a glimpse of how life could be different, through the visit to my aunt. He began to show me what it felt like to be loved and cared for. God clearly ignored all my opinions and my ignorance about Him and began working in my life despite me.

God's light—later, much later—illuminated His Word for me, so that I could continue to learn and grow in my understanding. This lambent light is everywhere, as is God. Hard hearts cause us to miss opportunities, but God changes that by giving us new hearts and new spirits.

I want to add here something that I feel is important. Many Christians will voice that we all have an empty place in our hearts that can only be filled by God. This implies that everyone either responds to this empty place, or ignores it. I do not know the answer to this, but I do know that I was never looking for God. Not once did I question topics of what I would consider a religious nature. I just got on with my life. I have told you that I thought the Pope was pompous. That must have come about since we received our first television when I was about nine years old. I don't know what the news was at that time concerning the Pope, but clearly, I formed an opinion about him.

As you read on, you will learn about some occurrences that happened to me that, for a long time, were completely inexplicable—so much so that I kept them to myself. Yet I always wondered about them. These events were truly extraordinary to me. There was that lighthouse beam again, sending directional clues. Yet even though I could not see them, I was compelled to follow the beams of light to where God wanted me.

CHAPTER 7

And the lessons kept coming

During my training at a hospital in London, I first started to notice strange things. God was busy, at times, flashing that lighthouse ray, yet I could not see it. I was on my own path, making my own decisions, as I had been all my life.

The hospital served part of the east end of London, an area that was then a predominantly poor and crime-ridden area. At that time, the Kray twins lived in that area. They were serious criminals who once appeared on my ward, late at night, to visit a patient whose jaw they had fractured while robbing the patient's lorry. It turns out that the patient was part of the gang. But I digress.

The children at the school for the disabled were under the care of this hospital. Having visited the hospital whenever I was asked to accompany a child from the school, I had determined that this was where I wished to train. I did not, however, have the entry requirements, as I had left school before entering the sixth form and had no A-level qualifications. At that time in England, children sat Ordinary Level (O-level) exams at sixteen and Advanced Level (A-level) exams at eighteen if they stayed on at school into the sixth form (the English school level for sixteen to seventeen year-olds). I went ahead and applied anyway. I was interviewed, given an IQ test, and accepted. Who would have thought? Everyone else had been required to have eight O-levels and three A-levels. I was far from that.

I also did not have any money. On my first day, I watched parents bringing their daughters to the induction day, and writing checks to pay for the pile of textbooks and file paper allotted to each student. Of course, I was not the first student to be in that position, so I was allowed to gradually pay the bill from my meagre salary.

During our initial three months of training, we were called probationers and we received only classroom teaching. Not everyone fared well. People left for various reasons; some simply failed the exams, some decided nursing was not for them, some were considered too overweight and had been unable to reduce, and some were asked to leave. Our numbers were halved by the time we were starting to visit the wards.

At this hospital, I met Mary, my first proper Christian. At that time, I considered her a proper Christian because she did more than just attend church. She was our set leader. Mary was a little older than the rest of us, and she was a true believer in Christ. As our set leader, she had the job of passing down any instructions or messages from the administration to the group. We became good friends, but how she ever found the grace to tolerate my outspoken opinions and views, I do not know.

When students lit candles at their churches before exams, I mocked them; when they prayed for me, I mocked them more, angry and offended that they thought I needed prayer, as if I were somehow deficient in some way. They prayed anyway.

I did well during my training. I learned quickly, thanks to excellent teaching. I left school knowing I had less qualifications than my peers. As I started at this hospital, I found myself so intensely interested in what made people ill and what could be done about it, that I was like a sponge soaking in every little fact. I loved my work. As I look back and see how unworthy I was to be in that situation, I am so thankful to God, a God who required nothing from me. As

I said right in the beginning, there was a long time before I knew who God was.

Our teaching constantly reinforced the idea that we wereto put the patient first. One day I was tidying the enormous linen cupboard. We called it a cupboard, yet it was bigger than my bedroom at home. I was feeling very virtuous about taking on this task without having been directed to it. Pride is a wonderful thing. The matron came to the ward, doing a round, as we called it back then. She found me. Instead of praising me, she put me in my place. Why was I not sitting with a particular patient who seemed to be the only one without visitors? I had to get to him.

Unlike many other hospitals, we were encouraged to sit with patients. To begin with, I found it hard to trust this idea. There were always jobs that needed doing, and yet to just stop and sit with a patient seemed to be a misplaced luxury. It was a recognition that our work was for people and those people were God's people. This was a continuation of the principles of the Christian founders.

Every day, a nurse would kneel in the ward and read a prayer out loud. I made it very clear that this would not be something I would want to do. The Christian approach did not end when that nurse finished the reading. The patients were the priority. The care was toward their physical, mental, and spiritual health—only I did not know about spiritual health yet. Learning to make the patient's need a priority was a necessary but humbling lesson. This not only shaped me as a nurse but as a person. I learned to foresee needs, learned to listen, learned the power of touch, learned to let people cry, learned the difference between sympathy and empathy, and most important of all, I learned to let the patient retain control and dignity.

And the lessons kept coming. We had a system of blue books. These were books filled with procedures that we had to have signed by a qualified nurse once she deemed us competent. Most of my colleagues found this process stressful, but I seemed to work through each section easily. We were taught to do things as shown. No deviation was allowed and no short cuts. There was a set place for every instrument on every procedure trolley we had to prepare. A trolley existed for every procedure. One day I was paired with a doctor to assist him with a patient, and because I knew the doctor was left-handed, I had moved the blood pressure machine on the trolley to make it more convenient for him. Helpful Ash here? Wrong again. I was reprimanded severely. Sometimes I felt I could do no right for doing wrong. This was very humbling at the time, but years later in a different environment, I was surprisingly asked to prepare for a particular procedure for a doctor in his surgery, and I could still remember how to do it. This level of attention to detail felt demanding, and sometimes too rigid, yet it did the trick.

CHAPTER 8

Who wants to go to church?

The lessons continued off the ward. Later in our training, we were moved into a newly built nurses' home. Two rooms shared a common bathroom, and Mary and I were paired up.

One particular night, it was dark and cold and seriously stormy. I was getting ready to meet my boyfriend while Mary was dressing for church. I suddenly realized how bad the weather was and asked Mary if she thought going to church was a good idea. Her reply stopped me in my tracks. She said, "Does it occur to you that I *want* to go to church?" Well no, it had not occurred to me. Who *wants* to go to church? I couldn't get my head around someone who would go out in that weather for church. After all, I was about to go out with my boyfriend and enjoy myself. That made sense. My boyfriend could drive as he was old enough, but we could not. But as Mary left to go to church, I could not see why she would endure the weather, and public transport, just for that. Clearly, I saw church as a place to endure.

Paul said it right in Philippians 2:3: "Do nothing from selfish ambition or conceit, but in humility count others more significant than yourselves." This was the message of my training.

Our training was certainly a lesson in humility. Each unit in the hospital was a ward that specialized in either surgery or medicine or even specific diagnoses. The old building had what were called Nightingale wards. The wards had two sections of beds down each side of each wall, separated only by heavy curtains that blocked vision but not sounds. There was very little privacy but much community. The newer part of the building had sections with six beds. Every ward had side rooms for single patients who might be infectious, or who were more frail. The wards that only cared for patients with tuberculosis actually closed shortly after I started my training, as the advances in treatment meant people did not require admission to hospital. Our longevity as students set our hierarchy in the system. Students on their first wards were the lowest of the low, and as one progressed, one's standing increased. This was not designed to impede one in any way but was actually a protection. The expectation was that we would do as we were told and taught. At first, all questions from the patients were given the response, "I will ask Sister for you." Even when we knew things, we were expected not to assume we could answer.

Then, as we developed seniority, we also had to protect those below. I was learning to communicate, and I was catching up on social norms. I was learning from everybody about their lives, which were very different from mine, and trying to believe that it really was possible to live with a different set of expectations.

Thus far in my life, I had not purposefully lied about anything. What I mean, I suppose, is that telling lies was not my default button. Why do people lie? Maybe because they are scared. I did not lie, and yet I had learned somehow that I would not be believed. I cannot think of an incident that caused this, yet somehow I had no expectation that I would automatically be believed because I said something. This next incident brought that home to me.

My first ward was a female surgical ward. In my first few days, I was given a 1–10 duty. That meant I would be on duty at 1:00 p.m. and off duty at 10:00 p.m. I overslept and was late reporting to the staff nurse in charge. I apologized and the staff nurse accepted, without batting an eyelid. The next time I had the same shift, I overslept, confessed, and my apology was again accepted.

A few days later, it happened a third time. As I rushed to the ward, I was trying to invent a plausible reason. Surely the truth would not work a third time without some imagined punishment. When I arrived at the ward, all I could say was the truth and apologize. It impressed me to no end that I was believed a third time. I expected not to be believed and to be punished in some way. As I was recounting this to Mary, I learned that the Staff Nurse was another believer.

This expression *believer* was the way Mary described all those who went to church with her. I never asked her why she used this term—another thing that passed me by. I had noticed that Mary had a different language, and I now see that in church for myself. Mary was never lucky, but often blessed. Her church friends were believers, never Christians, or Catholics, or Methodists. There were so many new things that I just accepted, as if I was coming out of a shell of non-communication at home and into a world with many new languages, new ways, and new foods.

The way I had been treated by that staff nurse, was the way I was expected to treat others. In fact, this was part of a broader pattern. We were never told we were doing wrong but always asked, instead, if what we were doing would benefit the patient. Once I was found drinking orange juice in the ward kitchen; we were only allowed water.

The ward sister appeared and at my back I heard, "Tell me, nurse, how that will benefit the patients?"

By the time I turned around to those piercing eyes, I had invented my answer: "I was dehydrated and would not be thinking clearly without a drink and I drank orange juice so I could drink a sufficient amount more quickly and return to the ward." I knew I had been reprimanded for drinking orange juice and she knew I knew. This was the pattern. As I said, we were never told we were wrong in a direct way. This was the way we were constantly taught to put the patient first. I had broken a rule about not using supplies for my own use. The sister could have just told me that, but she made me think of the patients. I had not told a lie either. That light around me was not just a prompter but an illuminator to my thoughts. But I had years to go before I saw it.

Nobody would have believed how my childhood had been, or so I thought. Many of my colleagues had been much more privileged than I had. Abuse was not spoken of until the case of a little girl who lived near the hospital became headline news. It seemed that the world was ready to hear that parents could harm their own children and even cause their deaths. I think that the lighthouse from God helped me to keep to the truth—if not keep to the truth, then to keep silent. How right was Isaiah when he gave us God's message that "my thoughts are not your thoughts" (Isaiah 55:8a).

This next story shows how blind I was to God's light. Despite what happened, I still did not recognize that God's hand was with me. This happened in my second year of training.

CHAPTER 9

As long as I could hear him breathe

Due to much sickness among staff at the hospital, I was asked to fill in and take charge of one of the children's wards for the night. This was an exceedingly special circumstance. The hospital had a staffing crisis due to an infectious disease spreading rapidly. I was promised a special, speedy backup should I need it. All that would be required was for me to dial just one number on the ward telephone.

This was no walk-in-the-park duty. This ward was a Nightingale ward and of course, at night, the ward is much darker. The lights are dimmed and one has a portable torch (flashlight) to carry for close-up work. Everybody tries to be as quiet as possible so that the children may sleep. Some children had had surgery that day. There was a little boy with a serious condition of either croup or diphtheria. I was to wait for a consultant to come to ascertain the correct diagnosis for this little boy.

Imagine this. On the boy's bedside locker sat a tracheotomy set. If his breathing stopped, I was to cut open his trachea, insert a breathing tube, and wait for help to arrive. The amazing thing was that I actually knew how to do it. His breathing was labored and noisy, and wherever I was, I could hear him. As long as I could hear him breathe, I could breathe. Suddenly the consultant arrived. It was past midnight. He was wearing a cape and was dressed in a tuxedo. He stood at the entrance to the ward, in all his pomp and grandeur.

He did not introduce himself. He did not appear to care that I was even there, or that anybody else was even there. He just shouted in a deep roar, "There is no diphtheria here. I cannot smell diphtheria. You young 'uns will never know that smell. And people will die!" He spun on his heel and left. Such a drama queen. So my little charge had croup. I would not be operating on him that night.

As the night progressed, and all appeared well, the time came when I could take my meal break. The staff room was a short walk away. I was all ready to settle with my coffee and my crossword puzzle, yet I didn't even get to sit down. For some reason, I returned to the ward. I still don't know why. There was no thought in my head that I needed to return. Nothing was concerning me. There were no nagging thoughts, and no anxieties. Furthermore, I didn't even ask myself why I was returning. I was compelled. Here was God's lambent light guiding me back—a bright light I could not see.

I headed straight for one of the side wards where a student was caring for a baby who had had surgery that day. He was being nursed on a crucifix splint so that his tiny limbs could not interfere with the wound on his abdomen. As I looked in through the window, I saw that the nurse was giving him a bottle. This was not an easy task with a baby in such a splint. The child's face was black. The fluid was going into his lungs. The nurse had not noticed. There was a ward telephone right where I was. This was wonderful, since not all rooms had the bell that near. I pressed the special number, which I had been given earlier, and within seconds help arrived. I rushed to an adjoining ward to fetch a portable suction machine. His tiny lungs were cleared. He was saved. He breathed normally. I asked that same nurse to continue with his feeding, and we noticed together that her habit was to watch that the level was going down in the feeding bottle. This would show that the baby was strong enough to suck—something we have to check—but should not take the place of checking the baby's color. Many mothers can fall into this trap too with strong, healthy babies.

This child was the son of a vicar. Naturally, I wonder what

became of him. However, until I was saved, I never knew why I returned to that ward and went straight to that baby. It mystified me and became a secret that I could not share. If I ever told the story, colleagues would assume that being in charge as a junior nurse had obviously given me anxieties. Only I knew that was not the way it was. God needed me to save that life. Just because I did not know God did not change God's plan for that baby. This makes me believe that when God wants us to know something, or to do something, He will make it happen. That baby's life was not dependent on my knowing God, but rather on God knowing what God wanted. God does not change. God used me to save that baby despite my not knowing Him. This is a theological concept that tells us that God shows grace to all mankind.

I quoted Isaiah earlier and that next verse goes on to say, "For as the heavens are higher than the earth, so are my ways higher than your ways and my thoughts than your thoughts" (Isaiah 55:9). The only reason I can now tell these stories is because I have faith in God. Things I chose to keep a secret were explained as soon as I was saved. It is awe-inspiring to me to have experienced this incident with the baby. I had been an instrument for God. Having said that though, I still feel hesitant to relate these things because there are people seeking miracles in all things. If people get better from an illness, I hear a miracle being claimed. There is such a difference between a miracle and God's providence. God puts people in the right place at the right time for His own glory.

If you find it difficult to believe this happened the way I have written it, then you are going to have difficulty with the rest of the things I want to say. Maybe reading 1 Corinthians 12:8 will help: "For to one is given through the Spirit the utterance of wisdom, and to another the utterance of knowledge according to the same Spirit."

CHAPTER 10

I faced some rocky times

Throughout my training, I gradually came to understand that we all learn differently. There were areas in my training that I struggled with more than others did, and I started to note the different ways teachers explained things. One night this was brought home to me in spades. The night sister approached me to ask if I could help a more senior student by having her as an extra pair of hands. She had failed her finals more than once and there was, at that time, a limit to the number of times one could sit the exams. I was asked if I could assess her in some way.

When she arrived, I was about to start the drug round, giving out medications to all the patients. I asked her to do the bottle round. Her task was to collect each urinal from every male patient, record the amount of urine passed, and do any chemical testing investigations so ordered. This task was at the level of a first warder. It never occurred to me that it was beyond her ability. In fact, I had thought she might object to being given a task beneath her status. There was a clue there.

Though she followed through with the task without complaint, I saw I had overestimated her. She had collected all the urinals, emptied them without any measurements or investigations, and placed them in the sterilizing unit. I was dumbstruck. This nurse had knowledge far beyond me when it came to theory, but practically she was totally unable to perform well. She had an extraordinary mind, but I do not know how she had got this far and still remained in training. I have no idea what happened to her, but the experience sowed a seed and increased my interest in enabling people to learn.

Looking back, I see that God had plans for my entire life—if only I had seen His beams of light beckoning me toward His way. What a patient God we have. My life moved on and I faced some rocky times, yet there was still a phenomenon that to this day I do not fully grasp.

Just to orient you to the time in my life, I will tell you that I married the man I had dated throughout my training. He was in the army, and once I had qualified, I joined him in Malaya, in the Far East. After only twenty months we returned to England, as my husband had become a commissioned officer. We lived in various places but eventually settled and my two sons started school. This enabled me to return to work.

Here is my problem. I cannot explain adequately how to convince you about something that I came to recognize. Sometimes I know things that have no foundation in my sphere of experiences or knowledge. This is another thing I have not talked about very much. When I have mentioned it, people find an explanation that is not valid. So I am asking you to accept, as I have to, that while this makes no sense at all, sometimes I know things that I cannot possibly have any clue about.

This only became evident to me once I returned to work, but it is not restricted to work matters. For instance, one day my youngest son, then just seven years old, displayed exactly the same thing to me, in that he spoke of knowing something he could not know. He came home from school in such a rage. He was so out of control that I just dumped him in the bath fully dressed and turned the taps on. As he calmed down, I was able to ask why he was so angry. He had been forbidden to answer questions in class because he had known too many of the answers. "Every time she opens her mouth, I know what she is going to say," he told me. He threw an enormous sponge up in the air and it hit the lamp, sending sparks everywhere. I felt, in an instant, a total understanding—a goosebump moment. He told me his teacher was asking about Egypt, and, stupidly, I asked how he knew anything about Egypt. Up went the sponge again. In instant rage, he declared he did not know how he knew.

There is more to tell about this, but this is not the place. This just added fuel to what God had already started in me: a fascination with how people learn. This thing I have about knowing things is both a blessing and a difficulty. Often, I have to keep quiet, otherwise I sound opinionated, or I am told I am just intuitive. It is neither, and I know the difference. I have given up trying to fathom it. My son, however, thinks that if he finds things simple, then everyone else does too. Therefore, he concludes that any lack of understanding just means they are being obstructive.

I could conclude that, for me, this is a blessing from God. In fact, that is all I must conclude. Each time it happened, I was unsure how to use it. That still applies today. Now, though, if it happens, I can pray for guidance.

There was another lesson coming. Once my children started school I worked as a practice nurse for a group of doctors. This role was covered by two nurses. Our work involved dealing with minor injuries, as they presented, and assisting with vaccinations and other tasks, as directed by the doctors. I loved that position but increasingly became concerned that maybe I needed to update my nursing knowledge.

I accepted a position in a local hospital as a liaison nurse. A liaison nurse bridges the gaps that can occur between the different professions for the benefit of the patient. The liaison nurse keeps each profession, and the family, up to date with the care being received by any individual, and any specialist support needed. I decided to do a further degree course in advanced nursing, since I assumed that the length of time away from hospital care must mean I would need to be updated on the new drugs and new practices.

I nearly gave up in the first year. One of the topics was cell structure, which by itself is illuminating. The idea is if you know the cell, you can get folk well. However, for some reason, we were coterminously growing tomato plants. I could not grasp how the tomato plants related to the topic. And if I am honest, I cared not. I gave this as the reason for giving up, but was told that I was the only one who was willing to ask questions, and that the others also wanted the same answers as I did. Since I have never had a hang-up about asking questions, I had not realized that many do. This just fed my interest in understanding learning. I managed to finish that course and went on to do a course for teaching adults. I became a clinical nurse teacher. My specialties covered wound care, infection control, and care of the elderly. This position allowed me to work on the wards, alongside the nurses, teaching and demonstrating high standards of care.

Look how this scripture fits my story. Isaiah 46:10b states that "my counsel shall stand, and I will accomplish all my purpose."

CHAPTER 11

Potential area of difficulty

Over time, as health care in England began to change in major ways, my problematic predictions came to the fore, one after the other. Examples may bore you, but I will try to put you in the picture. We suddenly had many changes in management. Many of the new managers had no clue about health care, and they kept coming up with new ideas but could not see why they would not work. One man decided to try some weird idea for easing communication. He would tell three colleagues any news item and they were each given a group of six to spread the message to. Those then each had a group of six and so on until a person became informed that he or she was in a group and must attend a meeting at a set time and day each week. At this meeting, no questions were allowed. One just had to listen. Attendance was demanded. I pointed out that the nurses had different rotations each week, and would not be coming in to work to listen to a message that could be sent by a memo. I never attended a meeting, giving the same reason each time. The idea was abandoned but not before I was branded as negative. To counteract this I decided to change my language. Instead of saying that whatever was being proposed would be a problem, I changed to saying it would create "a potential area of difficulty." This seemed more positive in that it hinted at a solution. It has to be said that the changes being implemented flew in the face of care.

Suddenly, new, non-medical managers were being appointed who knew the cost of everything and the value of nothing. It was hard to remain silent. If we needed equipment to care for wounds, all that was seen was the cost of the equipment; the fact that the patient's suffering would be reduced was secondary, as would their length of stay. It was hard.

A new role was created for each department in the hospital, and I was appointed to that position for elderly care. Creating a new role from a job description is not always easy, but again, God was good in that I was with a manager who allowed me the freedom to work it out. Other managers had set ideas about the shape of the role and set the determinations. In elderly care, the purpose of the role was to improve the standard of care and to improve recruitment to an unpopular area of nursing. I was able to achieve both by first teaching an accredited course on elderly care and making the role of the nurse more satisfying. Within the year, we had a waiting list of nurses wishing to transfer to the department.

The manager and I appointed a new ward sister, and I designed her induction. The ward sister is in charge of her patients and her nursing staff. One day, I was on her ward discussing something when we walked past a side room. The door was slightly ajar, not open enough to see more than the foot of the bed. Continuing to talk to her, I walked into that room and found, at the head of the bed, that the air mattress was unplugged. Of course, I just plugged it back in, and we continued our discussion. Because the plug was on the back wall, there was no way I could have seen it was unplugged. That sister asked me how I knew, and I had no idea. How could I?

It did not end there. A short time later, I was on that same ward helping that same sister to make a bed ready to receive a patient back from surgery. Suddenly, for no apparent reason, I crossed the ward to a patient, drew the curtains around his bed and pressed the crash bell. As I did that, the patient collapsed. The resuscitation team arrived almost immediately, and the man was revived. Again, it was a mystery to me how I knew that was all going to happen.

The patient showed no signs and no distress, yet had a sudden heart attack. The effect on this ward sister was to see me as some sort of wonder woman. What a wonderful witness that would have been if I had been aware of the existence of God in my life.

It is worth repeating Isaiah 46:10: "my counsel shall stand, and I will accomplish all my purpose." But God knew. That is the only way I can explain things now. I was still not a believer and now I regret that I did not find out what these patients went on to do. I so wish I had. There is no need for me to know for sure that God had a plan for their lives too, just as He had for mine.

With God in my life, my frustrations would have been better handled. I was full on busy: starting a new job, being diagnosed with lupus, studying for a master's degree, and getting divorced. After twenty-three years of marriage, when my sons were in their teens, I left my husband. It was a spur of the moment decision, which is not the best way to do it. It was based on many reasons, but totally unplanned. Without that lambent light, all would have been lost.

CHAPTER 12

I thought I had it all to do— that I was on my own

One day I went to work with my car packed up to the hilt, expecting to spend the night in the car park at the hospital. I had nowhere to go. Fortunately, I was given hospital accommodation, but I did not receive that news until 4:00 p.m. that day. My divorce was so unpleasant that my lawyer had to have counselling. My husband's lawyer was very abusive to her. I felt that I needed the counselling more than she did, however, so I found it hard to be sympathetic. I was not advised well by my lawyer, and I was too naïve. I just wanted out of the marriage, and I thought a lawyer would direct my path better than I would on my own. I did not get a fair settlement. This was made very clear when I changed my lawyer part way through.

Throughout this time, I was able to function at work, but as soon as I was on my own, I just sank into a dark despair. Two of my students, Sally and Cath, both believers, would keep watch on me. They would cook things, offer to shop, or sometimes just call for a short chat through the window. I must have seemed very ungrateful because my responses were limited.

I was financially vulnerable, and my teenage sons were living in our house with their father. We had a big house, but it would not sell. I discovered that my husband had placed the sale in the hands of a friend who was making no effort since it benefitted my husband to stay there. I became a lodger with a colleague. My lawyer seemed unable to do anything about all this and I was in limbo. Finally, the divorce went through. My new lawyer was limited in what she could do at this stage, but she did find a few thousand pounds that had been hidden from me.

I thought I had it all to do—that I was on my own. God's lighthouse was still shining my way. There came a serious slump in the housing market. It was sad for some, but it enabled me to afford a mortgage and buy my own house. My sons had also moved out and found their own accommodation. I thought I was just lucky. I was on my way to accomplishing God's purpose in my life, but I was so ignorant of that.

Life during this time was not completely dreary. Much joy came through my work. I was able to design a new way of nursing that changed the focus of care from task-oriented to patient-centered care. There were many models of nursing being written, and I was able to see how to apply them. Until then, nurses had no idea that they were task-oriented. Everyone just followed what went on before. The new ideas were so extreme that they were hard to comprehend, so most people did not try. We had to shift our focus from doing *for* the patient to helping them care for themselves. It is a more rehabilitative way of thinking—a very different approach that now seems the obvious way to do things. This approach, of course, gives the patient more control and choice. I designed a new way to implement this philosophy and, of course, teach it. I saw this as my skill—nothing to do with God—and took pride in the recognition I received. As you read on, be prepared for weird and strange things to happen.

PART 3

CHAPTER 13

Who will know their names?

Following the continuation of a huge reorganization of the National Health Service in England, I took on a role as manager of a hospital in a different county. It had crumbled into a mass of chaotic nonsensical practices, and I had it all to do, from sorting out the ordering and storage, to training the staff, to managing the care contract and the multidisciplinary team. My title was manager, but I was in sole charge and still a registered nurse. The hospital was basically being used as a long-term residence for people waiting to die. It had to be returned to an acute admitting hospital. The patients were identified by the new Health Service as bed-blockers. I found that so against all I had been taught. I chose to call them GUeSts, which stood for "Got Unexpected Stay." After all, it was not their fault that they were there.

The care at the hospital was stabilized and we had the staff all working together as a team implementing the many developments. I decided that I could take a holiday. Little did I know that a dolphin would be my next messenger.

I went to Florida with a friend and we visited one of the theme parks. We were listening to one of the dolphin trainers explain how they cared for the sick dolphins. He told the crowd that to live, dolphins must keep on the move. If they stopped moving, all their dolphin friends would nudge them along until they were independent again. As I heard this, a window opened in my brain. I was far from work and not even thinking about the hospital. But quite suddenly, I could see a new way forward to help the patients. When I returned, it took a very short time to plan our next moves. The Dolphin Project was born. Basically, we were going to stop doing all the things we had been doing for patients which they in fact could still do for themselves. I expected hurdles because quite honestly many patients enjoy being patients and having everything done for them.

The date we commenced this sea-change, it was the night staff's responsibility to implement it. Those patients who were able would be told they could serve themselves breakfast in the dining room. The nurses cared for those who needed help and thus could spend more time with them. A nurse supervised the activity in the dining room, where patients were making their own toast and pouring their own tea from individual pots. One patient complained. All the others were thrilled to have fresh toast and hot tea. We had been unaware that serving a whole ward made the food substandard. As a result of changes like this, we found patients could be discharged sooner and with more confidence in their own abilities.

To my surprise, I discovered we had a patient who was misdiagnosed and had been allowed to live in the hospital. She would dictate who would care for her, when they would care for her, and what they would or would not do for her. As we changed the dynamics of care, she was causing the nurses great difficulties. She would be upset if the nurses prioritized acute care needs over hers. This came to my attention, and I discovered the lady had Munchausen Syndrome.

Munchausen Syndrome was named in 1951 after Baron Munchausen, who lived in the eighteenth century, and whose name had become proverbial as a narrator of falsely exaggerated exploits. In politically correct arenas, it is now called factitious disorder. It is used to describe people who act as if they are ill, when in fact they are not. This lady was acting as if she was totally paralyzed from the neck down. One of her stories was that she had been badly burned in a house fire while saving the people living there, yet she had no burn scars.

There were many other stories that were not difficult to investigate, and I was surprised that everybody had accepted all her symptoms as genuine. Of course, staff had seen her moving when she thought no one was looking but had hesitated to say anything. As I said, long story short: I decided we needed to achieve a better quality of life for her and hopefully find assisted living accommodation for her. We devised a multi-disciplinary approach that actually involved every member of staff, including the office staff and ancillary workers. We met her only brother and his wife and shared our plan. They were delighted that their own thoughts were validated.

We set a start date.

It was clear this lady would need an advocate because from the start date onwards, everyone she met would be thwarting her every wish. She would need someone to speak for her. I asked the local vicar if he would be that advocate and he agreed. Neil, the vicar, was also our part-time hospital chaplain, and we would meet regularly. He would plead a request from the patient and I would either deny it or, on rare occasions, negotiate a compromise.

Then one day, in my office, Neil said something to me—I wish I could remember what it was—but my reply was, "You have to remember I do not believe all that rubbish in the Bible. I think we have to be good and kind, but—"

Before I could finish, he stood up, seeming a bit ruffled (really, who could blame him?). As he turned, he said "Ash, I'm sure you love your sons, but who will know their names in two thousand years' time?" And he left.

My first thought was to wonder, *What is the matter with him?* Then I turned back to my desk to carry on with whatever I had been working on—except I could no longer focus. He was right. No one would know my sons' names in two thousand years.

It seems strange as I tell it here. My every thought was, *He's right about that.* Driving to work and home again, the same thought repeated itself like a mantra. On the following Friday, when Neil appeared at my office door, I told him not to come in. He took a step forward. I told him again, and added that I had had no peace since Tuesday. Little did I realize what I was saying. To my horror, he invited me to lunch the following day. My head was screaming no, but my mouth said yes.

Jeremiah 5:21 describes my state at this time: "Hear this, Oh foolish and senseless people, who have eyes, but see not, who have ears, but hear not." God decided to try a new way to get my attention. Neil was only the forerunner.

CHAPTER 14

You don't have to understand

The dinners with Neil continued and every objection I raised about the Bible stories (as I knew them), elicited a response from Neil. Never did he tell me what I should think, or what it meant. His reply was always, "This is how I see it," and I found myself constantly thinking that how he saw it was reasonable. Reasonable? What a word to use. Reasonable. There is a touch of arrogance there, though of course I did not see it at the time. This was me.

For reasons that will bore you, I left the Health Service. I no longer wanted to be a part of it. However, even after I left, Neil and I remained connected. I had begun reading many books which he gave me, even books I did not like, such as one about the saints, worshipped by the Catholics. Yet I read everything, approaching the task like an obedient child doing homework, as if it was a chore with no real reason to it beyond getting it done.

I had decided that being retired and no longer working was not to be. A former staff nurse contacted me to see if I would go to Switzerland to manage a ski company that she and her husband had started. She was still at the hospital, and her husband had a full-time position. I agreed to go, wondering what on earth I knew about managing a ski company. I still don't know.

Neil told me to buy a Bible and gave me something called *Read Mark and Build*. I have since learned that this was a daily devotional, but at the time it looked like a small booklet that a child of five could read. The idea was that I would read the daily section of Mark followed by the commentary. I had free time every afternoon to lie on the grass and do this job. I need to confess my attitude here. I noticed two things happened every time I picked up my Bible in the chalet where I was living. The first thing was that I was not embarrassed to be picking up a Bible. What was that all about? Obviously, I expected to be. The second thing I have to confess is that every time I did pick up the Bible, the action triggered a smile. Now here is the confession. Me being me, I tried not to smile. I could not avoid it. This was weird to me. I was naturally happy, but this particular smile occurred involuntarily, whether I wanted it or not. Why smile because you have picked up a Bible?

There I was each afternoon, lying on the grass, halfway up a mountain, God's beauty on full display. To my right were snow scenes, with the mountain climbing to the sky. To my left was lush grass and budding crocuses down in the valley. This was where I read through the gospel of Mark.

When I reached the part about divorce, I spoke to the grass out loud. I had not expected to be divorced and the words I was reading seemed accusatory and unfair. Then I reached the story of the death of Jesus. I read this. I did not understand it. I could not see why such a fuss was made at Easter. If Jesus were real, then surely the fact that He had been born was the big deal, not His death. Again, I talked to the grass. "I don't understand this," I said. I heard a voice say, "You don't have to understand; just accept."

Without looking around, or even wondering where that voice came from, I replied that I could just accept it. I immediately half-ran, half-walked down the mountain to the nearest telephone to tell Neil that I thought I had just become a Christian.

It was a long time later that I realized I had heard a voice and not even searched for the source. I heard a voice! It was not in my head. It was audible. And yet, it takes me awhile sometimes to question things. I smile as I write this, because it is so like me to miss the main point. God had actually spoken to me. It was not the last time. Matthew 4:19 says, "And He said to them, 'Follow me, and I will make you fishers of men.'" I saw Neil as a "fisher of men."

Though I cannot remember how he reacted when I gave him this stunning news of my acceptance of Christ and His Words, I recollect that it was a very short, matter-of-fact conversation. Neither of us praised the Lord.

PART 4

CHAPTER 15

God required me to catch up

By this time, I had been divorced for about fifteen years. I saw my eldest son infrequently and my youngest more often. I decided that I needed to work again. Correction: I had a clue from my bank account that I needed to work again. After I returned from Switzerland, I started to work part-time in nursing homes. I then received a call from my friend Mary, who had been our set leader at the hospital in London where we trained. She was concerned for the future of a nursing home in Kent, where her parents had been living until they passed. I was living in Dorset at the time, and she wanted to know if I would be interested in managing the nursing home in Kent. Kent is a four- to six-hour drive from my house. How could that work?

Well, if it is part of God's plan, He has a way already for it to work. I drove up to meet with Mary and the new future owner. The home was owned by a missionary society and needed to be brought up to the required standards of care. Many years earlier, the house had been sold to the mission for a tiny sum. Since then, it had been run by former missionaries as a place for those missionaries returning from abroad to retire. At this time, the society wanted to sell it, as it was running at a loss, but were apparently not allowed to sell it for that very reason.

The mission had the services of a man who already owned

another home. He offered to make it a financial success. At this time, all the residents were former missionaries. There were also six small flats within the grounds for missionaries who were physically independent but of limited means. The complex of flats had a guest room which became my accommodation once I accepted the position of nurse manager. This position became a master class in Christianity. God required me to catch up.

Shortly after I arrived, I received a call from the night nurse to tell me she had found another job and would not be back. I had no nurse for the coming night. I called every nursing agency, every current staff member, all to no avail. I prayed. I told God that I could work that day and stay on for the night, but I would not be able to also be there for the following day. This was a problem. If I could not get a night nurse by noon that same day, then I knew I would most certainly not get one at all. I was concerned. Clearly, I thought God needed a warning.

Living in one of the flats was a tiny lady called Betty. She suddenly appeared at my side in the corridor and observed that I looked worried. I told her I was worried. She told me to "give it to God." I snapped back that I had given it to God. She calmly told me that I obviously hadn't because I was still worried. I was fit to commit murder. This woman, I thought, had no idea how the world ran. I walked into my office and literally threw my arms up in the air, saying, "God, take it." I had done all I could. Then I went for a long, slow walk around the grounds. I admired the grass, the flowers, and the trees. Here I was, finally, admiring God's creation. I never gave the problem another thought. After a long break, I returned to my desk and worked.

At 4:50 p.m. I said out loud to God, "Okay, I have the message. I am working tonight, but I have no idea what is going to happen tomorrow." Listen to me. Hilarious!

At that point, the telephone rang. A voice said, "Hello, I am a nurse looking for work." Chills! I asked if she could work that night.

She said she could. More chills! We faced a challenge to get her to find where we were, but she accepted and was on her way.

That is how I learned what it means to "give it to God." You have to let it go and wait for God to do whatever He is going to do. When the nurse arrived, the staff called me and I returned to give her a full handover. Her knowledge and manner impressed me. I felt I had left everyone in safe hands. She had my number and could call me at any time. When I returned in the morning, she had left me a lovely note saying how she had enjoyed her shift and would have loved to work for me full time, but could not because of the commute. Thank you, God. God just never leaves us. His lambent light is around us. He taught me to let go of my problem by finding something else to do and totally focusing on that. It has been a wonderful lesson learned.

This light for me now is not the flashing beams of a lighthouse. Now that He has my attention, it is a gentle flickering light encouraging me to remember I am His child and He is there.

There is a rider to this story. Once I had the night nurse problem, solved I rushed to Betty's flat. I told her the whole story—even that I had had murderous thoughts—and I kept saying how amazing this was. Betty was not reacting. I think I wanted her to jump up and down, or grab my hands and dance. Instead she just carried on preparing her supper—a flat response. Exasperated, I asked her why she was not amazed. She simply said, "It is not amazing, dear, it is wonderful. We have a wonderful God and we should not be surprised." Would I ever learn?

CHAPTER 16

But—it was a big but

All the time I was at that nursing home, I was being taught and learning about God. I had not been there very long when I was informed that the inspectors were going to visit. This was very daunting and could have serious repercussions if we were at fault. I was new to this, and I was concerned on many fronts. I knew we were on a journey and had not yet fulfilled all the requirements to meet regulations. My main concern, however, was that through being so new to the home, I would not always have the full answer to any question, thereby letting the staff down by answering incorrectly. I shared this with one of the missionaries. Later that night, a slip of paper was pushed under the door of my room in the onsite flats. It was a text from Matthew 10:19-20: "When they deliver you over, do not be anxious how you are to speak or what you are to say, for what you are to say will be given to you in that hour. For it is not you who speak, but the Spirit of your Father speaking through you." The lambent light.

By the time the next inspection came around, I had made positive changes and introduced care plans. I had also taught the staff about the many forms of dementia and how to describe the behaviors in a more useful way than just to say a person is "confused." Little did I know how timely that instruction had been.

For this next inspection, a new idea had been introduced

whereby lay people would also inspect alongside the official. Lay people were interested volunteers who had no medical knowledge and were independent of the authorities or of the homeowners. It was felt, by the Inspecting Authority, that they could bring a keener eye to the situation. Sounds like a plan, doesn't it?

On this particular day, the volunteer was a man who objected to a picture of the Lord hanging on the wall and accused me of brainwashing the staff. I directed him to talk to our cook, who was not a Christian, and ask her how she felt. Was she ever forced to attend any prayer meeting or religious service? Later, after talking to some residents, he returned to me and accused me of placing a resident's bed on the grass outside, at supper time, and making her stay there as a punishment. I told him he had been talking to a confused lady. He was not convinced. I fetched her notes and, fortunately, my teaching had been put into practice. The nurse had written that the lady was confused about time, manner, and place. Not content with that victory, I then made the man come to her room with me. I showed him how difficult it was to strip a bed completely, then dismantle it into its four parts, carry each heavy awkward part outside, rebuild it, remake the bed, and somehow convince the resident to get in and stay in—all at a busy supper time. I was not amused but the inspector was, and the idea of using volunteers was abandoned shortly afterwards. I was still a relatively immature Christian, but the residents there taught me so much. God had me in His hand, for sure.

We had a lady resident who was always complaining. It was impossible to please her. It was a very sad situation to see someone who loved the Lord but did not like her life. She had not been a missionary but was a self-professed Christian. She read her Bible and Christian literature. One day, a nurse called Sylvia, who had been caring for this lady, came to my office in tears. Something this lady had said against her had really upset her. We talked about it and prayed together.

The next day, the nurse arrived with a gift for this lady. She had taken the trouble to find something she knew the resident would particularly like. I was amazed. That nurse taught me that we are to love everyone, not just the nice people. I had so much to learn, but God was transforming me. God put lambent lights in my path and does to this day. The more I grow spiritually, the more I see Him. That candle flickers in view so much more often. When I read 1 John 3:18—"Little children, let us not love in word or talk but in deed and in truth"—I think of that nurse. She did not buy that gift as some sort of appeasement. She bought it to show love, and that made the difference. We do not have to like everyone, but we do have to love everyone.

There was a nursing sister who moved away. She was a former missionary. I had a great deal of respect for all the staff, but especially her. I asked a favor of her. I asked if she would critique my work with a view to see how it impacted the lives of the residents. I knew any criticism would be worth hearing. A couple of months later, her letter arrived and I read it. Tears flowed immediately. She gave a glowing account of how much better was the care for the residents, *but*—it was a big *but*—she told me I thought I was doing well in my own strength.

She told me that God's hand was directing me, and only because God was in control was any development being successfully implemented. The tears came instantly, but they were tears of joy. I was convicted. I knew she was right. Suddenly, I understood that without God, we are nothing and can do nothing. What a gift she gave me. I prayed with gratitude for the letter, the lesson, and my salvation.

This was the moment it came together. I finally began to see that God had been in my life for years, that all the good things that had happened to me were from Him. For the first time, I really felt as if someone was taking care of me. It was a good feeling. As a result of this revelation, I began to talk to God. I began to ask Him for direction. I now knew with a certainty that He would answer. I knew I was not achieving in my own strength. This was both humbling and joyful. I had been so blind. It was like taking a picture with a phone that now could take panoramic videos.

Further, I also learned that I had become someone who did not ask for things. As a child, I had seen that asking never prompted a response. Thus, I grew up never asking. Even having recognized this, I still struggle to this day with asking for help from people. Can you believe when my children were small, I struggled to ask for people to babysit? It's such a common expectation from mothers of small children, yet not for me. Thank God, I can ask God. Psalm 9:1 says, "I will give thanks to the LORD, with all my whole heart; I will recount all of your wonderful deeds." There are so many reasons to give thanks and even to see God fixing someone else.

Yet though I now absolutely believed that God could and did answer prayers, at this time in my life, I sometimes still struggled to accept it, even when the evidence was undeniable.

CHAPTER 17

I was skeptical

Take, for instance, what happened with Betty. I met her earlier when she told me to "give it to God." Betty was a tiny lady, even shorter than me. I came to nickname her "a walking saint." Betty still lived independently. She had macular degeneration, and her sight was failing dramatically. This upset her so much because she could not bear the thought of losing her sight, but thought she ought to be able to bear it. She cried out to God. She confessed to the minister of our church, and the elders anointed her with oil and prayed for her vision to be restored. And it was.

Not immediately, but within a few days, Betty came to tell me that she could see. I was skeptical. I rang a friend, with whom I had trained and who actually worked in the very eye department that Betty visited locally, to give her the news. My friend reacted the same way I had. We both felt we would need to read her medical notes. Betty's ophthalmologist, also a Christian, had believed Betty when she told him she could see, but not perfectly but enough to get by. Betty would regularly invite me to dinner, and I started to watch and notice that Betty did, in fact, see, but somehow differently. I cannot find a way to explain or describe what I saw. Betty somehow could see without looking. I would stare and stare at her, and yet not fathom how she was seeing. She could not see dust on the furniture but could safely walk the six miles into the nearest town to shop. She could see her money. She could read again. Macular degeneration is a progressive eye disease, which meant her eyesight should be deteriorating, not improving. Yet God had been at work.

God had helped Betty for sure, but would it be arrogant of me to wonder if He wanted me to see this in order to strengthen my faith? If God did this for Betty, would He not do it for anyone to further His plan and to give Him the glory? Of course He would. God opens the eyes of the blind, both metaphorically and literally, because to paraphrase Psalm 146:17, God loves the righteous, and Betty was righteous. She was also bowed down, and He lifted her up.

I was soon to hear that voice again. God was going to speak to me. Who would have thought?

Before I had gone to the nursing home in Kent, I had been going to different churches near my house. After six months or so, I had not settled anywhere. After arrival at the home, I had started to go to church with Betty. I had been so welcomed by all the people there. This church felt very different than any I had previously attended. I was reminded of my friend Mary, when I realized every Sunday I wanted to be there. She would laugh.

One day a lady was speaking of her testimony prior to her baptism, and she explained that she had decided to be baptized as an act of obedience to God. I mulled on this. It had never occurred to me that baptism was an act of obedience. I had been baptized as a child, but I had not been involved in that at all. As I thought more, I felt I needed to make a public declaration of my faith. One evening, while dining with friends, I shared that I was thinking of being baptized. I was nearly dunked, there and then, in the upstairs bathroom! I had not fully made up my mind, but I was definitely encouraged that night. I called Neil, and he was not pleased; he reminded me that I had already been christened as a baby. I replied that I did not think God would mind. That was the extent of the phone call.

I was baptized on Easter Sunday 2003. I had been a Christian for about four or five years. After the event, I was given a tape recording of the service. In my flat later that same afternoon, I replayed the tape. An extraordinary thing happened. I suddenly felt as if I was being filled with air. I felt as if I was being blown up to twice my size. I was breathing as if I had too much air—more than I could cope with. I had no idea what was happening to me. Just as I reached a level of panic I heard that same voice for a second time. All that was said was, "I am pleased."

I had a complete feeling of warmth, and joy and peace. I felt as if I was glowing. I have never shared this experience. As fast as this began, so it ended. It is strange to say that it was enough for me to hear those words. I then told nobody and just carried on with whatever I was doing. How differently I would react today after such an event. I would definitely share this.

Perhaps we do not talk enough about the way God works in our lives. I don't know. I was aware that I knew the voice to be of God. I had a certainty of that. That too still seems unusual. But it happened. This became another secret. My reaction was to know that something good had happened. It was all mine. In my limited experience of being a believer, I just thought this was not believable. After all, it is so difficult to even describe. I now have read that Ephesians tells us to be "filled with the Spirit" (Ephesians 5:18b). I have never heard anyone else talk of a similar thing. Are we all keeping it to ourselves?

There's a fear that others will think I am overly spiritual, that I need some drama in my life, or that I think I am extra special in God's eyes. All these things are in the way of me telling my story. More likely, it is because I expect the rest of the world to be as skeptical as I can be.

Before I move on to the next part of my story, I feel the need to talk about this voice a little more. Now I have been brave enough to confess all. As a nurse, I know some people hear voices. I want to explain why my voice is not the same. I am no expert on mental illness, but I do know that the voices heard by patients are a problem because they cause harm to the patient in some way. They are reported to be as audible as mine is, but they are of a negative nature. They are words that any reasonable person would question or object to. They are humiliating or hostile. Despite this, they appear to be equally compelling. Of course, I recognize how we all interpret things differently. I also am aware that I never questioned the voice each time I heard it. All I can say is that I somehow just had a certainty that it was from God. And would God ever leave us in doubt?

CHAPTER 18

This is bold for England

My work at the nursing home in Kent seemed to come to a stage where I could easily leave and hand the work over to another. It began to seem ridiculous to be paying a mortgage for a home in Dorset but rarely living there. Moving back home would mean I would need to find a new church, and I was not very confident that I would find one as good as the one I was attending in Kent. As I prepared to leave, someone told me about a church fairly near to my house, but I did not know exactly where it was. Once home, I visited many churches, travelling farther and farther afield with no joy. I was seeking that same welcome I had experienced in Kent. I told you I can be slow; well, finally, I made an effort to find the church I had been told about. It was nearer than I thought. I parked the car one Saturday morning and walked across to the notice board to discover the times of the service. The building was a Church of England church but it was shared by a Baptist church. As I found the Baptist service times, I heard that voice simply say, "This is it." I keep stressing how unusual I knew it to be, to hear a voice like this. This was the third time it happened. I just accepted it, carried on, and gave thanks to God.

God's lambent light was with me as the next day I pulled into the car park, shared by the shopping complex nearby. As I was getting out of my car, another car parked beside me, and a man got out. Very boldly, I asked if he was going into the church. He replied that he was and again, very boldly, I asked if I could walk in with him. This is bold for England. Anyway, he introduced himself as the minister. Well, of course he was—God knew my needs. The minister introduced me to a friendly lady who helped me to meet others and invited me to dinner. I should have known, maybe, that God wanted me at this church all along. And maybe if I had followed through when I was first told about it, I would have joined sooner. Genesis 28:15 says, "'Behold, I am with you and will keep you wherever you go, and will bring you back to this land. For I will not leave you until I have done what I have promised you.'"

These voices were not something I expected to hear, nor did I ask God to speak to me. Each time they delivered a short message. All I knew was that the messages were from God. God did not introduce himself, but He gave me the sense to recognize Him. I knew I was not imagining them. They were audible rather than just thoughts. They did not bother me in any way. The voices could be trusted. I never knew when I would hear one but there were more to come.

As time passed, and as I grew in my walk with the Lord, I became troubled by the fact that I could not forgive my father for the sex abuse I had suffered at home as a child. I had come to learn that this was very wrong. God had not only forgiven me for my past sins but would continue to accept my repentance for future sins. This would continue until I was in His presence and then sin would be absent.

CHAPTER 19

I want to want to

I prayed constantly, asking to forgive my father. I mean, year after year, this was my prayer. I confessed this to one of the church leaders and we prayed about it. Quite by chance, Neil was in the area and he invited me to lunch. We were sitting in a cozy pub enjoying our lunch, and I felt able to tell Neil about the abuse and my inability to forgive. Neil suggested that my prayer should really be that I *want* to forgive my father. Immediately, I saw that he was right. The truth was I did not want to forgive my father. I was so pleased to recognize this. However, as soon as I said so, Neil said no, the prayer should be that I *want* to *want* to. I saw it. If forgiveness was on a scale of one to ten, then maybe I was at minus one hundred.

I was far from forgiveness. I had to want to want to forgive. This was such a gift, because I totally understood how far away I was. From then on, day in, day out, while I was vacuuming, driving, or doing the laundry, I would pray to want to want to. I perceived no change, but I knew I was sincere in my efforts. And then one day, I heard that voice. I was heading for the kitchen to make a coffee and the voice just said, "You don't have to do this anymore." I suddenly felt a weight go from my shoulders, a weight I had not perceived that I was carrying. But I felt physically lighter. I knew the voice. I knew I did not need to pray about this ever again. Here's the thing: I also had not forgiven my father and yet somehow, I was to leave this with

God. I have never prayed about it since, and I carry no guilt. It is as if this forgiveness has been done for me. That explanation seems inadequate. It was exactly as if a light had been switched on for me. I know forgiveness is a hard thing for many people, and forgetting is even harder. However, God took all this from me in an instant. He gave me peace about this. How amazing is that? Oops! Sorry Betty. It is wonderful. It is wonderful.

To this day, I do not know how to answer the question about whether I have forgiven my father. I have done nothing, but I have had a clear message to do no more. I have to let the theologians ponder this one. All I can do is tell you what happened, and what God did for me. For me, I sometimes need to reorder words to grasp the meaning, and maybe that is the same for you. I see the word *forgiveness* as a phrase. I think of it this way: the situation (that needs forgiveness) exists so that it can be given (for giving) to God. The hurt is there in order to give it to God because we cannot deal with it. Maybe we overcomplicate forgiveness. Really our problem is with the difficulty of forgetting. I know that if we cannot forget, then maybe we have given it to God but not let go. I have found it helpful to see the word *forgiveness* differently.

CHAPTER 20

The loss of identity is hard to observe

I had continued to manage nursing care homes when I left Kent. When this next incident occurred, I was working fairly locally for a corporation. They owned several homes and none of them were places where I would want to live. Of course, when I took the position, all I knew was that the home needed a lot of TLC. The home badly needed redecoration, and I failed to achieve that. The place had been run as if it was a warehouse, where the residents were fed and watered. There was no individualized care; in fact, there was very little real care, just routines and policies to follow. Too late I came to realize that the company did not want a manager. They just needed someone who could obey instructions, implement pre-written policies, and have no creativity at all.

The residents with dementia ate in a separate dining room, as their behaviors were thought to be too upsetting for the other residents to witness. To this end, their meals were served as slops, meaning their first soup course was poured on their dinner to make it fluid enough to be spooned into their mouths. Who does this? Horrific. I could write so much about this sort of thing. The people were not being treated as human beings, but rather as work objects. Elderly care really does need a crusader. It is easy to fix, but of course fixing it costs. People I meet say they do not want to go into a nursing home. Why is that? There is a clue there. The loss of dignity is hard to watch. The loss of identity is hard to observe. I also challenge relatives to remember that their loved one is still a person and does not need to be restrained to prevent the person from falling. I want to see the term *wanderer* banned. People choose to walk at inappropriate times to inappropriate places. Their purpose is to walk, and to move, and they should be assisted in doing this safely, not be restrained from it. All these things describe only one small aspect of institutional care. This place I found myself in was dehumanizing and the staff could not see it. Every place I worked required me to change the way care was delivered.

I saw people routinely strapped to their beds because, it was alleged, they would fall out of bed. If I asked when it last happened, nobody would know. Then you would see that new admissions would be strapped down. Skin care was not seen to be important. No one asked what people's normal routines were. No face creams were used, so the skin became dry and sore. Teeth were not cleaned as it is not easy to clean someone else's teeth, and even more difficult if he or she is unable to work with you. Women were shaved and left with stubble.

Incontinence pads were rationed, and when replaced, there was no washing of the area between changes. If anyone started to shout out he or she was medicated before anyone bothered to see if the person had pain, or toothache, or was frightened, or anything else. There were no treats—just meals. There were no meaningful activities. No wonder nobody wants to wake up in a nursing home. It need not be this way. It should not be this way.

With God's help, I endured the sight of things that should not have happened. There were so many small actions that dehumanized people—actions that are simple to avoid. For example, if someone was in a wheelchair and it was time to take the person somewhere else, there was no interaction or explanation given and no warning that suddenly the person was going to be moved. I find this sort of thing uncaring and thoughtless. Care assistants would call out to their colleagues, in front of all the residents, if someone had been incontinent and they were about to deal with it. It was as if everyone was deaf and blind. I knew I could teach ways to change these things, but it would take time to end the suffering.

The start of my demise began when I decided to get the dining room for those with dementia redecorated. I had banned the staff from smoking anywhere and everywhere, and I had stopped the soup being used to liquidize the food. Small goals. The décor was dirty and dull and I wanted this dining room to be an attractive place in which to be. I approached local companies for provisions to improve this room, and they were very responsive and generous. Stupidly, I thought the organization that I worked for would be pleased, but they were very displeased. However, they did not tell me that at the time. What they did some weeks later was to ask me to go home and not return until I heard from them. I was shocked—so shocked that I immediately contacted my church minister. By the time I reached home, I had convinced myself that I had done something wrong, only I did not know what it was. I kept running everything through my head, but I could not come up with any reason that would cause me to be sent home.

CHAPTER 21

All will be well

By the end of that day, I had decided that I would wake in the morning remembering what I had done, only that did not happen. I was totally convinced that I must have done something really bad. It was strange that I could not recall what it was. I was supported by a friend from church who kept urging me to contact my professional body. Finally I did, but not until I had received a date for a disciplinary hearing.

My professional body was, in fact, a trade union that provided the necessary public liability insurance for nurses. The general secretary of my professional body herself heard my tale of woe, and came all the way from London to meet me at my home. She brought someone with her who also listened to my story. I subsequently learned that this man was famous in the trade union world, and it was his belief that I had done nothing, despite my insistence that I must have done something. I gave him permission to represent me, and he took over. He changed the date of the disciplinary hearing to one more convenient to himself. When that morning came, I was staring out of my window onto my garden. I had worked out that I would need a new job, since whatever the outcome, there was no way I wanted to work for these people again. Of course, I could not imagine there would be a favorable outcome, so how would I be able to convince a new employer to take me on?

As I was pondering on all these thoughts, I heard that voice again. This time it simply said, "All will be well." Instantly I knew all would be well. I had learned to trust that voice. I did not know how it would work out, but I now had a certainty that God was in this with me. Proverbs 3: 5 says, "Trust in the Lord with all your heart, and do not lean on your own understanding."

Lambent light.

The meeting started with the company personnel feeling disadvantaged by who was representing me. It seemed they were trying to accuse me of using the computer inappropriately during work time. I was told to just answer questions factually and to leave the rest to Mr. Union Man.

Suddenly, in response to something a company staff member said, he raised his voice and bellowed at her. Up until then, he had been very quietly-spoken and mild-mannered. He firmly put her in her place and then noted his credentials. He reminded them of the correct application of employment law. He asked for a recess and we were given a room to ourselves. Can you believe we opened the window and talked to each other with our heads outside "in case the phones were bugged"? He asked me if I wanted my job back, and of course I did not, and I was happy to leave everything else to him.

We returned to the meeting and he proceeded to quote chapter and verse to them about employment law and my rights and their errors. Again, suddenly, I was listening to a discussion about how much compensation the company should pay me for the insult of the suspension from employment for no valid reason. I had no idea I would come away richer and able to apply for other work with no blemish on my CV. I left that place and, while I waited for a generous check, I looked for other work. God is just. God is merciful.

To the time of writing, I have not heard the voice from God again, but in many other ways God has continued to get my attention.

CHAPTER 22

A directive from God

It was 2003 when I took my last nursing role, in another nursing home. I had by now retired four times, and I only went for an interview to this home because the agency that persisted in head-hunting me promised to stop calling if I would meet the owners. Well!

When I met them, I was so impressed with the care they were delivering, and the role they wanted me to take that I found myself agreeing to very part-time work. In fact, they agreed to me working out my own hours. The position was teaching and monitoring the quality of care actually delivered. I was able to implement new ideas and I loved it.

At last, I was working for people who were trying to do things the best way they knew how. Together, we developed two very different specialties. Both were government initiatives. The first initiative was end-of-life care. The idea of this was to encourage young and old people to become more interested in planning the end of their lives and thinking about their needs and desires, while they were still competent enough to do so. Within the nursing home, our role was to reexamine how we dealt with end-of-life care and how we could help family and friends to be more involved at this time.

The work was immensely rewarding. We had thought we were already doing a good job, but there were many nuances we decided to adopt to improve what we were doing. We took time to talk to families about the life histories of our residents. Usually we had only learned about these when we attended funerals for our people. It was illuminating and helped the junior staff to see the residents as people who had functioned well in their fitter years.

The next big push from the government was about well-being. The government wanted organizations to make inroads to ensure their workplaces looked after the well-being of their staff. I was sent to a conference and again learned so much. I was very much a fan of well-being, and in the light of what subsequently happened, I am now passionate for all Christians to understand how to achieve well-being.

This was God preparing me for what was to come. I had no idea that God would use this knowledge I had in the way that He did. This is why I am so keen for every Christian to see His lambent light. I think we know that God is always with us. He tells us so. But do we have a real sense of His presence as we tend to our daily agendas and routines?

The conference on well-being endorsed all that I had already learned but added aspects that, though small, impacted me greatly. I learned that certain plants enhance well-being. Here's the thing. Many kitchen cabinets and other furniture are made from MDF; here in the States, I think it is called particle board. This product gives off harmful chemicals. There are plants that absorb these chemicals; one of them is Gerbera daisies. Here is what amazes me. God made those plants, with those abilities, long before we learned how to make particle board. God goes before. See Isaiah 45:2a, which says, "I will go before you." Betty, my lady in Kent, was right again. We should not be amazed. It is wonderful what God does.

One Sunday, I was in church when a lady with stage four bone cancer gave a testimony. She described how she had just been discharged from the local hospice where she had been admitted for pain control. While there, she found another patient screaming with pain. This lady got out of her bed, went to the other lady, and sat with her. I sat listening to this in awe, knowing that if it had been me, I probably would not be helping someone else. I probably would have been so wrapped up in my own problems that I am not convinced I would have been thinking of anyone else. It was, for me, a powerful testimony.

During that same service, the minister asked the deacons to stand around the sides of the church to receive people for prayer. He often did this. I was joined by a fellow deacon, and to my horror, I saw a lady heading for us. My judgmental thoughts immediately came to the fore and I was sending arrow prayers of apology to God. This lady had been coming for prayer ever since I had joined the church. She was always overcome by her problems, but was unable to do anything to help herself. People would get alongside her and be drained by her. We prayed for her often, and on this day my colleague and I prayed with her.

Driving home, I received what I can only call a directive from God. I felt I was told to call her and offer to help. I parked the car, I went straight into my house and dialed her number on the phone. I could hardly believe what I was saying. I told her she was thirty-eight years old, and I was then sixty-eight years old. I asked if she intended to keep on doing what she was doing for the next thirty years! I put an exclamation mark there because I could hardly believe what I was saying. I told her I could help her. My head was saying to me, *Who do you think you are?* I had no idea how I could help her. She burst into tears and said she needed help. I told her she had to want it. (I really did say that!) She said she did want it. I told her we would meet in a week and I would explain the plan (the plan that did not exist), and if she wanted to go forward, we would arrange meetings. Her name was Anna and we arranged an initial meeting.

God did not let go of me. I made a cup of coffee, but not before God had directed me to select three or four books I had and my Bible. Four hours later, I had a six-week program outlined. There was no way I could have done that in my own strength. Anyone who is a teacher is cognizant of how long it takes to prepare a lesson. This would normally have taken me much longer. Also, God showed me which scriptures to use. I was not so familiar with the Bible that I could find scriptures that easily. They were not new to me, but if you had asked me, I would not have known from which book they were in.

I needed someone else to be present to be able to have the scriptures found ahead of time so that there was no interruption to the flow. The person God gave me was Angie, and she was perfect. She is a very godly woman and knew when to interject and when to keep silent. She knew where to find her scriptures. She also understood confidentiality.

CHAPTER 23

On eagles' wings

The first week arrived and, as planned, Anna walked in. She looked downtrodden and had an air of defeat. There was no joy in her. She was also a nurse, which made communication easier. We ended the session and Anna left assuring us she would be back the following week. Angie and I prayed.

The following week, Anna had changed. Her head was up, her eyes seemed bright, and she greeted both Angie and me with such a smile that we had to comment. It seemed as if Anna had taken one step and God had lifted her up on eagles' wings. It was such an encouraging moment. Anna had done the homework and she had prayed for herself. She shared that she had a sense that everything was going to be okay. The sessions continued as God showed me how to help her, and He showed her how to respond and change her brain worms, as I call them.

What a joy God gave Angie and me as we saw her healing transformation.

Anna completed the sessions and had a new spring in her step. Our church was celebrating Maundy Thursday with a dinner in a private room of a local organization in our town. As people were arriving, we were all milling around and chatting. Suddenly the room went quiet because Anna walked in. She looked stunning!

She had ditched the childish hairstyle and become a sophisticated, beautiful woman.

Everyone was so pleased for her and the joy she received from their acclamations was so precious. This was such a witness to the way God works in our lives. Anna subsequently shared her story with the church and went on to be promoted at work because of her new-found confidence, positive attitude, and improved self-esteem.

CHAPTER 24

As your day, so shall your strength be

My story does not end here, but my journey to Florida and decision to become a permanent resident belongs elsewhere. This has been a short book about things that I realized happened with God at the wheel—things that He brought about even though I had no knowledge or interest in Him. His lambent light has definitely shone throughout my entire life. God has protected me and directed me, and finally called me to be his adopted child.

In the story of Abraham in Genesis 22:5, Abraham is leaving to take his son to be sacrificed because God told him to do this. Abraham says to his companions, "'stay here with the donkey; I and the boy will go over there and worship and come again to you.'" He does not say *I* will be back. He says that *he and the boy* will be back. This is so encouraging. Abraham had no clue about what God was going to do—just as we do now. When we are faced with problems that seem unsurmountable, we can think of Abraham and we can know that God will sort it out.

I have come to understand that there are times when we need to recognize that God can be silent. God is sovereign and there is no obligation for Him to answer us, inform us, or indeed, to let us know anything. As I write this, we are in the middle of the COVID pandemic. None of us knows what is going on, and none of us knows how this will play out. But what we do know is that God is in control and He will make things clear for us when He decides He wants to.

Sometimes any long silence from God can be like sitting with a friend in a room in silence; saying nothing but being content and at peace. The time comes, of course, when we have to come out of that room anyway. We have to go on with whatever busyness we are choosing to do. We can do this knowing God is at work, knowing that He holds us in His hands; we have to trust and obey, confident that His plans for us will work out for the glory of God.

God wants us to take that first step sometimes, and then He has our backs. He does lift us up as if on eagles' wings and we fly forward. I hope this book encourages every reader to start to notice that lambent light of God, ever present in their lives.

Sometimes I come to the end of a story and having enjoyed the book, I find the ending disappointing, or deflating, and I find it colors my opinion about the book. The enjoyment I have had vanishes somewhat. I think there is a lesson in that too. We cannot judge our story by what is our current situation, because our current situation is not our ending. As believers, we know our ending is victory. We need the scripture of Job to remember we can live in confidence until our time on earth is done.

God found a way for me to connect with Him. He did the same for the Israelites. In Exodus, we learn that both God and the Israelites wanted things to go back to the way they were in the Garden of Eden, but sin got in the way. God continues now to find a way for each one of us.

I started this book by saying there was a time when I did not know God. It was a long time too. However, look how God has saved me from myself. Has always been around me, and still is that flickering, glowing light, whether I see it or not. The more I read His Word, the closer I get in my walk with Him.

As I said at the beginning, when I made the decision to make a last visit to my son in America, I never dreamt that I would be here for good. As always, God had more plans for me and has continued to help me see that lambent light—the obvious proof that He lives in me.

I would like to leave you with part of Jesus's prayer from John 17:24-26.

> "Father, I desire that they also, whom you have given me, may be with me where I am, to see my glory you have given me because you loved me before the foundation of the world. O Righteous Father, even though the world does not know you, I know you, and these know that you have sent me. I made known to them your name, and I will continue to make it known, that with which you have loved me may be in them, and I in them."

Thank you for reading my story, and I extend that to all those in my list of acknowledgments who helped me to write. I would be interested in any comments or questions that you may have, so do not hesitate to get in touch.

The End

READER'S GUIDE AND DISCUSSION QUESTIONS

While the topics below are separate and can lead to broader issues, they also are interlinked throughout the book. The writer invites you to share your thoughts within a group of readers.

Topic One: Sex abuse

NB: Before addressing this topic it is necessary for the leader to be aware that someone in the group may have been a victim of sex abuse, or may be related to, or know, a perpetrator. In preparation, have available the contact details for any local resource that may be able to offer help and support. The term *sex abuse* is preferred from *sexual abuse*, since *sexual* usually is used when describing something desirable, rather than abuse or rape or incest.

1. Why is this topic difficult to talk about?
2. Why do we keep secrets as a child and as an adult?
3. As a community of faith, how does your church deal with this?
4. How should we protect our children? Would it make sense to teach our children about *good touch* and *bad touch* rather than *stranger danger*, since most perpetrators are known to the child or trusted by the child?

Prayer: Father God, it is a sad fact that many people worldwide are victims or perpetrators of sex abuse. We know the effects for a victim are deep-rooted. Help us to help any victims to be able to voice their pain and give them resources to help them. We also look for healing for both victims and perpetrators. Help us to remember that we are to love our enemies. Help us to remember that forgiveness is not about saying that actions against us no longer matter. Help us to learn how to respond and care for anyone who confides in us. Give us wisdom and guidance and courage to point them to Jesus. We ask all this in Jesus's name. Amen.

Topic Two: Church

1. Is church a habit or a need for you?
2. Is the church a family to you?
3. Why is coming to church an obstacle to overcome for some?
4. What is a way God has shown up in your life?

Prayer: Father God, we thank you that we can gather together to worship you as a faith community. Help us always to remember the love and hate of the cross: because you hate sin, you sent your only Son to take our sin so that we may be free. Thank you that you accepted the atonement. Thank you for our salvation. Help us to use the gifts you have given each of us in service to you. We give you the glory in all we do. In Jesus's holy name we pray. Amen.

Topic Three: Influence

1. Who has influenced you most to become who you are?
2. List all those who have impressed or inspired you.
3. Why is it important to have good influences?
4. Influence, as a power, can be good or bad. How do we discern the difference?

Prayer: Father God, we thank you for all those people who you put in our paths to teach us and direct us. We thank you for those who helped us know you. Help us Lord to be in your Word in order to know you more and be guided by your influence. Help us to be awake to the influence of culture on our spiritual lives. Protect us from negative influences and keep us from harm. We ask, too, that you guide us to be good influences and role models for others. In Jesus's name we pray. Amen.

BIBLIOGRAPHY

McCann, Rebecca. 1960. *Complete Cheerful Cherub*. New York: Crown Publishers Inc..

Printed in the United States
by Baker & Taylor Publisher Services